THE WALKMEN HAVE LANDE

Norman Silver was born in Cape Town, South Africa, in 1946. He moved to England in 1969, and has remained there, working in remand homes for adolescents, then teaching computer programming, before taking up writing full time. He lives with his family in Suffolk.

THE WALKMEN
HAVE LANDED

Norman Silver

faber and faber
LONDON · BOSTON

First published in 1994
by Faber and Faber Limited
3 Queen Square London WC1N 3AU

Photoset in Sabon by Wilmaset Ltd, Wirral
Printed in England by Clays Ltd, St Ives plc

A CIP record for this book is available from the British Library

ISBN 0-571-17189-3

10 9 8 7 6 5 4 3 2 1

Contents

I Want Trainers

that stand out in a crowd,
that mark you number one on the block,
that raise you off the concrete,
that stamp your identity on the streets,
that make your every footstep a dance,
that find their own way through town,
that magnetize the eyes of your mates,

with innersoles like trampolines,
with tongues that reach your knees,
with laces that hang loose,
with gold-plated lettering,
with treads deeper than tractor wheels,
with footprints that spell danger,
with hugely inflated price-tags,

because the way I am I'm a nonentity,
because even Sam has got a pair,
because you love me and you're my parents,
because feet need all the attention they can get,
because I'm suffering severe shoe envy,
because what I wear is what I am,
because if I don't get them I might as well be DEAD!

Dirty Song

Use the sea as a garbage-bin:
throw your dirty rubbish in,
    make a paste
    of industrial waste,
your petrol and your paraffin.
    The sea won't mind
    if it's not refined,
she'll take it all with a friendly grin.

Use the sea as a garbage-bin:
throw your heavy metals in.
    Your sewage too
    will help the brew –
she won't mind if it's thick or thin.
    Your plastic bags
    and blood-stained rags,
she'll clean the lot with a rinse and spin.

Use the sea as a garbage-bin:
throw your radiation in,
    your spare crude oils,
    your spills and spoils,
to her it's sweet as saccharine.
    Dump your trash
    without a splash,
she won't complain, she's a heroine.

Use the sea as a garbage-bin:
throw your toxic poisons in.
    The sea's too broad
    to be overawed
by a tiny drop of mortal sin.
    And if she dies
    who'll realize
that your love for her wasn't genuine?

Screen Champion

My world is a rectangle.
I'm shrunk to the size of a bat.
I move it to the left.
I move it to the right.

The ball bounces madly
around the treacherous court
until gravity makes it drop
to my jittery bat.

Either I make connection
or the ball falls out of sight.
Either the game continues
or I lose a precious life.

My world is a rectangle.
My body is the size of a bat.
I move it to the left.
I move it to the right.

The tension is exquisite.
My hand shivers with pleasure.
If fortune smiles on me
I am given a deadly laser

or the screen slows down
or the ball divides into three.
Sometimes the bat expands
or becomes sticky.

Perhaps I score extra points
by blasting away obstacles.
But best of all bonuses
is access to a higher level:

to discover a fresh maze
with a wicked set of challenges,
swarming with creatures
and intriguing dangers.

My world is a rectangle.
This little bat is everything I am.
I move it to the left.
I move it to the right.

I dream of this bat
in the secrecy of night.
The tension is exquisite.
My hand shivers with pleasure.

Even to die is glorious:
a brief musical acclaim
followed by three new lives
in which to perfect my aim.

If I ever top a million
my name will go up in lights.
I'll be forever inscribed
on the board of champions.

My world is a rectangle.
My body is the size of a bat.
I move it to the left.
I move it to the right.

Only to the left or right.
I shiver with pleasure.

Medicine Bag

In my medicine bag
is brave Grandfather's old watch
with its worn leather strap,
a woollen purple glove
that keeps Mother warm in winter,
a metal spanner
from Father's tool-kit
which he uses for repairs,
a wound-up guitar string
that belonged to singing Elder Brother,
twelve loose hairs from Sheba's tail
because she barks so loudly,
and the book of riddles
that Mrs Bazra gave me.

The medicine bag
is made from Suki's scarf.
Suki's my best friend
and she's not afraid of anything.
The lace that you pull
to fasten the bag
is from Younger Sister's trainer.
She doesn't have worries yet.

I keep this medicine bag
with me in bed.
It gives me power
to keep away nightmares.

Wet and Wild

On his birthday I go with Giles
for the afternoon to Aquafun.
There are turquoise pools
to swim in and an artificial sun
shines down on a beach of tiles.

At high tide he holds my hand
as we jump over monster waves.
Later, when they are turned
off he and I do bombdives
in the still waters of deep end.

We ride the White Rapids in a round
tractor tube, dangling our feet,
but soon we're tipped upside down
and scrape our knees on concrete.
We're lucky we don't drown.

After a soft-serve ice-cream
we decide to hazard the Kamikaze.
It takes us an age to climb
to the summit but Giles feels woozy
and refuses to go on the flume.

Then suddenly he decides he will,
and off we go, torpedoing
faster and faster, until
we're shot out of the echoing
pipe and Giles shouts: Brill!

As we dry off beside a flowerbed
with plastic ferns, a passer-by
stares at the disabled boy spread
out beside me on the towel, and I
yell: What's your problem, dickhead?

18 Certificate

Jason has often been warned
never to go down to the cellar
but on this particular night
when his family has gone out

and his mates in the front room
are all absorbed in the movie,
he creeps down the dark stairs,
opens the squeaking iron door,

pulls aside the cobwebbed curtain
spangled with hairy spiders
and enters the darkness cautiously,
only to trip over a human corpse

whose desiccated skin punctures
and a cockroach crawls out,
followed by a thousand others,
persuading Jason to cross swiftly

to the far side of the chamber
where he discovers under a table
a nest of slime constructed
with rib-cages and skulls

in which seven green polyps
have been ripening for centuries,
waiting for another live human
to foolishly enter their domain

and provide the host body
for their writhing larvae,
which at this very moment detach
themselves from the green eggs

and swarm greedily towards Jason
who backs off, lifts the lid
of an ancient stone sarcophagus
and climbs in, but is surprised

to find Lucy already there,
with the werewolf's fang marks
in her delicate silky neck,
her eyes glazed with terror

(he thought he hadn't seen her
lately and this explained it),
and just as he guesses things
can't get very much worse,

Jason hears the chomping uproar
of the beast with three heads
as it rouses from its yearly nap
and stomps towards the stone box

flicking out its noxious tongues
and exuding anaesthetic gases
from an aperture beneath its tail,
but as it extends its claws

towards Jason, he leaps out,
leaving Lucy to be ripped apart,
and staggers towards the iron door
only to find himself face to face

with a specimen of the living dead
who is armed with dagger fingers
and has bad feelings towards boys
who disregard age-restrictions

on horror movies and gather to watch
hired videos in each other's houses,
so Jason is forced to act quickly,
and he does, shining his torch

directly into the vacant eyesockets
while uttering the oath: *I'm older
than I look*, at which the spectre
disintegrates into an ooze of jelly

and Jason manages to squeeze past
both the blob and the pathetic man
with the head of a fly who vomits
over his food before eating it,

and he dashes out the door,
up the dank flight of stairs
to the normality of his house
with its creamy floral wallpaper,

plump armchairs and tufty carpeting,
back to his mates in the front room
where he sits himself comfortably
just in time for THE END.

Life is a Ball

Nobody loves me,
no one at all.
To them it's a game
with me as the ball.

They kick me around
from one post to the other,
You know who I mean –
the old man and my mother.

I've tried to complain
but the linesman's blind.
He won't flag offside
when they're unkind.

Nobody cares
the way that I'm booted.
I've asked to be mended
or substituted.

But the crowd shouts:
Why are we waiting?
The coach doesn't bother
that my air's deflating.

Whether fair or foul
the game continues,
till my leather's worn
to its bare sinews.

I feel the bruises
and constant thuds,
as they thump me
with their metal studs.

They don't get sent off,
they don't get dismissal,
My only hope
is the referee's whistle.

Changes

Once the rivers were ballads
    but now they're forgotten music.
Once the tiger was an emperor
    but now it's moth-eaten.
Once the whale was a metropolis
    but now it's a sunken city.
Once the trees were cathedrals
    but now they're without faith.
Once the Inuit was a survivor
    but now he's been thawed out.
Once the soil was a banquet
    but now it's forcefed.
Once the rain was a husband
    but now it's a gangster.
Once the world was a berry
    but now it's all thorns.

Gifts

Vusi slowly peels off the newspaper
with its decoration of headlines
about the footballer who was stabbed
and adverts for a mild shampoo.
His father has woken him with the gift.
Outside, in the African dawn, smoke
still hangs over the corrugated roofs
weighted down with stones and old tyres.

Brett has thought about his birthday
present for ages and knows it will be
a remote-controlled Porsche because
he's told his dad that's what he wants.
And when he wakes up, sure enough,
there on his bedside table, wrapped
in elegant purple paper with silver
ribbons is his Porsche-shaped gift.

Eagerly, the last layer of newspaper
is removed and his father says: Vusi,
my son, I myself made this for you.
The boy stares at the wire vehicle
which even has a wire steering-wheel
for turning the two front wheels.
And a thick wire as long as a stick
for pushing the car along the ground.

Brett rips off the outer wrapping
and his heart sinks when he sees it.
It's a Ferrari, and not the Porsche
he had specifically asked for.
He says, Thank you and his dad says,
Sorry, they were out of Porsches
but a Ferrari's just as good,
isn't it? and Brett says, Yes.

Vusi steers the car to the gravel
road where Wellington, his friend,
meets him to walk to school.
Each wheel has a hundred twists
of metal to make a springy tyre.
Vusi and Wellington take turns
driving the car around the weeds
and bumpy ditches alongside the road.

At school Brett tests the range
of his Ferrari at a hundred metres.
His mate Alistair is keen to check
its turning radius but misjudges
and crashes the vehicle into a wall.
The front headlight shatters, but
Brett's not bothered, it's a Ferrari
and really he wanted a Porsche.

Why Don't You

quit reading this poem
and go decorate a butterfly's wings?
Or entertain your bedroom
with a million soap-bubbles?

Why don't you build a bus-shelter
on a route that ought to exist?
Or make a flying kite
out of a wrecked automobile?

Or you could play music
on a single hair of someone you love?
Or paint shooting stars on the toenails
of someone who's sleeping?

Why not ask the corner shop
for a packet of assorted words?
Or make your own delicious poem
out of flour and water?

Why don't you perform a raindance
on your neighbours' doorstep?
Or cut their monstrous hedge
into the shape of a teapot?

Why not quit reading this poem
and teach the downhearted in traffic jams
to construct origami frogs?
Then watch them leap.

Frozen

Who threw that rock
onto the frozen lake
and made those cracks?

Are those mallard ducks
practising to be clowns
in an ice-circus?

Look at the breath
coming from my mouth
and making mist.

And the alder-trees
bowing under the weight
of their tinkling icicles.

A three-toed bird
has printed its lifestory
on a blank page.

I can see the clouds
looking at themselves
in a giant mirror.

And I hope the carp
are keeping warm
under their ice-blanket.

But where's the swan
that was so graceful
yesterday on the pond?

My Dog

My dog's colour is more than chocolate,
    her tail busier than a windmill,
    her tongue sloppier and lickier
    each time she comes to greet me.

My dog first thing in the morning
    is a volcano of yelping joy;
    when I come too slowly downstairs
    I hear her impatient love for me.

My dog takes me willingly for a walk,
    she pulls me on my leash
    to her favourite of all places:
    the field of a thousand smells.

My dog is jumpier than a pogo-stick,
    her leaps vertical in long grass,
    her eyes smiling as she pops up
    to see the world on the other side.

My dog's heart is ocean-wide,
    she forgives me for my tempers
    and herself is never downcast,
    each day being a brand new day.

My dog's sleeping is dreamy,
    her eyelids twitch as she roams
    through her twilight dogland
    chasing uncatchable butterflies.

My dog knows when she's misbehaved:
    she slinks tail-between-legs
    away from the guilty puddle
    and cries dry tears in the corner.

My dog is a crazy mixed-up dog,
    more mongrel than a zeedonk,
    but bristling with beauty:
    her personality is her pedigree.

Private Worlds

The Walkmen have landed:
    you can see them
as they bus or cycle
    or jog
receiving signals
    from their planet.
Also their fingers twitch
    to a secret beat.

Shortsighted Gran thought
    they were wearing
hearing aids, poor souls.
    So many
with the affliction
    nowadays.
When she is told,
    she begins to hear
the tss-ts-tsssss
    leaking
from their headphones
    in public places.
They're all listening
    to the same song,
aren't they?
    she remarks.

James and Ozzie
    in the back seat
hammer their ear-drums
    with heavy rock.
It's a battle of bands:
    Iron Maiden
versus Shakespears Sister.
    And both versus
the Pavarotti arias
    which Mum plays
so very loudly
    on the car radio.

At home when Mum's angry
    she borrows
Ozzie's personal stereo
    and disappears
for several hours
    into her own room,
emerging only after
    the operatics,
when she feels she's ready
    to start again.

Unmarried Beverley
    also has a headset:
she desperately pedals
    her exercise bike
in time to lovesongs.
    She's travelled
agonies of miles in search
    of romance.

With the perfect system –
    graphic equalizer,
dolby noise reduction,
    super bass –
what does Gino listen to?
    Uninterrupted
all-day ball-by-ball
    cricket commentary.

Chris has a compact disc
    digital audio
plus two more personal stereos
    which he always
carries around. Perhaps
    he has six ears.

Is Vanessa the only one
    without a Walkman?
So what! She enjoys
    the gentle art
of conversation.
    But eventually
she too wants the bolt
    of lightning
to flash from one ear
    to the other
as in the advertisement.
    She spends
her school holidays
    picking
four hundred punnets
    of strawberries

to buy her own machine.
        The journey home,
which used to be a bore,
        has now become
a movie with personalized
        soundtrack.

Unlike Vicky, who won't
        lend hers
because she'll catch
        nasty bugs
from other people's ears,
        Vanessa places
her new headphones
        across Gran's
threadbare lilac head
        and Gran finally
hears what the fuss
        has been about.
It's a river of sound,
        she says,
on which she floats
        as she samples
the man with the golden flute.
        At night,
to help her fall asleep,
        she shuts out
the noises of her pain
        and wakes,
still wearing earphones,
        at dawn.

Lester doesn't hear
       the bus coming.
The tape keeps winding
       from reel to reel
long after the wheels
       of his bike
come to a sudden stop.
       Nobody knows
which track precisely
       he was on
when the double-decker
       with its noisy engine
buckled and broke
       his limbs.

F.E.M.

Half the world is sleeping
　　while half the world's awake.
I think whoever made the world
　　made a big mistake.

Why did he want it ball-shaped
　　when he could have had it flat?
There'd be no need for gravity
　　but he didn't think of that.

We'd all live in one time-zone
　　if he hadn't made a blunder.
We'd all be equal here on top
　　with not a soul down under.

If you're in agreement
　　with these views then I suggest
that you join the Flat Earth Movement
　　to get the world compressed!

Snapshots

The globe thistle
    is a world just becoming
    is a band of jazz trumpeters
    is a bomb halfway through its explosion
    is the crest of an African crane.
The creeper on the fence
    is a backstage of electric cable
    is the head of a Rasta-man nodding in time to the wind
    is a hammock overflowing with legs
    is a climber hanging from a ledge.
The dead elm
    is a witch casting a spell of forgetting
    is a burst radio
    is a robot munching metal twiglets
    is a monument inscribed with names of rabbits.
The field of beet
    is the earth that hasn't shaved
    is a landminded battlefield
    is a candlewick bedspread
    is a herd of tortoises.
The crow
    is a tramp scavenging for fag-ends
    is a melancholy undertaker in coat and tails
    is a remote-controlled nun
    is a policeman investigating a crime.

The hosepipe in the bucket
    is the fuse leading from a detonator
    is a snake having a drink
    is a spaceman's helmet and air-tube
    is a patient having a blood transfusion.
The sun-lounger
    is a marquee for ants
    is a toboggan for red-hot dreamers
    is a dachshund straining on a leash
    is a sleeping stick insect.
The sun
    is a distress flare to passing galaxies
    is the tip of a glowing finger
    is an eye that can't be out-stared
    is a hole burnt in the sky.
The pylon in the distance
    is a needle with four threads
    is the skeleton of a giraffe
    is a lighthouse shining black beams in daylight
    is a melting climbing frame.
The electric mower
    is a dog with an oxygen tank on its back
    is an unstoppable chatterbox
    is a mechanical sheep
    is a snail having open-heart surgery.

Why Mrs Parry Gave Up Teaching

Our procession through school corridors
was watched by unmanageable crowds of kids

bored with pollination and photosynthesis.
We brought in a scent from the real world.

Four of us carried the branch into class,
one at each corner slowly mourning for it.

It was dressed like a bride in white veils
splashed with congratulations of confetti.

We laid it in state on the art-room table
and sketched it still bursting with life

while Mrs Parry addressed the nation:
she remembered when it was only this high

and the school had just been constructed.
What a shame to be struck in its prime!

She concluded her eulogy with kind words
about beauty being eternal and the scar

engraved on the trunk serving as epitaph.
She proposed we paint not only what we saw

but the forces of earth, air, sun, water
transforming a seed into a live sculpture

emblazoned with green leaf and blossom.
I mixed her words gently with watercolour,

and a ghostly image of the fallen branch
resurrected itself on my handmade paper.

Such calm, after the morning's hurricane —
interrupted by our headmaster gusting in.

He couldn't permit debris in the art-room.
It was the caretaker's function to clear up.

We had caused a disturbance, and, anyway,
cherry trees weren't on the curriculum.

The Great Destroyer vs. The Crooked Bill

It's going to be a real hot contest
I can tell you.

From my ringside seat I'll provide you
a blow by blow account.

There's the sound of the bell which starts
the sixteenth century.

The European moves in threateningly:
one blow to the head

with his wooden club and the unarmed
Dodo falls to the canvas.

A roar of applause rises from the crowd
of meat-hungry sailors,

even though the Dodo's flesh is bitter
and not very nourishing.

Round 2 and another Dodo enters the ring.
It weighs-in at fifty pounds.

Look at those pathetic wings, utterly
incapable of flight.

With no previous experience of predators,
the rotund dove

walks straight towards its executioner.
With a single jab

the European crushes the Dodo's skull.
What a fabulous fight!

The next Dodo waddles across the ring
to the far ropes.

Fat chance! The European bounds after it
and overtakes the bird

in two steps. Whack! Another Dodo
hits the deck.

And now it's 1680 and the final round
of this close battle.

The last living Dodo enters the arena.
And if I'm not mistaken

it's as tame and gentle as its predecessors!
What a lonely expression

on its face as it is clubbed to death.
It's a KO of the entire species.

From the ringside in Mauritius I wish you
a very pleasant evening.

Birth

From the windowsill
of our ancient cottage
I saw my brother born.

Outside were ponies,
their manes and tails
swirling in the wind.

My swing swayed empty
from the old willow:
it would have to wait.

My mum smiled at me
through her breathing.
Soon, she said, soon.

She lay fat belly up
on the broad pine bed
aching for the midwife.

Pass me a damp cloth,
she said, so I did.
She wiped her face.

The midwife phoned.
She had been delayed.
Would get to us later.

Mother pushed harder.
The baby's coming,
she said, and I saw

its head between
my mum's open thighs.
Then my dad arrived

just as the tiny body
came slithering out.
Its face was blue

for the first moment.
Then my dad lifted
the baby in his hands

and I heard it murmur.
It was alive, alive,
and pink as bathsoap!

Come meet your brother,
Dad said, so I climbed
down from the window

and touched my brother
with one of my fingers.
His hand was so small.

Each finger perfect,
with a tiny fingernail
delicately formed.

Baby was still joined
by the umbilical cord
to Mum when he opened

his curious eyes
for the first time.
He looked right at me.

The doctor came next.
He checked my brother
and my mum, and cut

the navel-string.
He didn't stay long.
After about an hour

the midwife arrived.
She kept apologizing
for being so late

and she praised Mum
and Dad (and me too)
for doing so well.

She washed my brother
and then weighed him.
She gave him to Mum

to have his first feed
of milk at her breast.
He seemed thirsty.

I went out to my swing
and tried to reach
the blue of the sky.

Excuse Me!

Can't someone else bring in the shopping?
    I'm talking
on the phone and I'm in my socks.
    It takes hours
to lace my boots and you know Gemma's
    a chatterbox.

There's no way I can wash the car
    right now
because I'm listening to the new
    Michael Jackson
album and it's too divine to interrupt.
    Won't later do?

I agree I'm on the rota for washing up
    but can't you
do this one just to give me a break?
    I think
I have a serious temperature.
    Or a stomach ache.

It's not my turn to do the hoovering.
    I'm halfway through
the chapter and the hero's nearly dead.
    I can't stop now –
it's the most thrilling novel
    I've ever read.

I know I promised to do the potatoes –
 but after
'Neighbours' and before 'Home and Away'.
 Can't food wait?
There's no law about eating early
 every day.

Sorry! No time to clear the table.
 I'm meeting
friends outside Spin Dizzy at eight.
 And if I
have to think up any more excuses
 I'll be late.

Lightning

I was awoken by a juddering
shock of thunder.

I ran to my father's room
hoping to huddle for a while.

But he leapt up and cheered:
The golden sea-horses are galloping!

He led me by the hand
into the field behind our house

and pointed to the ghosts
of snow-mountains floating overhead.

Suddenly the sky cracked open
and the light burst through.

There they go! my father shouted,
and swung me through the high grass.

They bolted and dashed wildly
across the vast plains of darkness.

Their veins flow with electricity,
my dad declared as he put me

on his shoulders for a clear view.
I looked up and was showered

with big drops of the wet night.
The next flash was blinding.

What a magnificent leap, my dad said.
Did you see its fiery eyes?

When the storm passed
I dried off and Dad settled me in my bed.

He told me a story
about a man and his friend who rode

the golden sea-horses to the end
of the universe and back.

Armour

This vest
I am wearing
is so wordproof

that nothing
you say
could possibly

hurt me
not even
if you call me

all the names
under the sun
or insult

my mother
not even
if you embarrass me

or try to make
a fool of me
in public.

Ouch!

This vest
must have
a hole in it.

From the Dark Forests

Words
              are exasperated
           with following
each other
              like prisoners
in leg-irons.
           They desire
to be set loose
              in the dancing
playgrounds
              of possibility.

Bored
with having
        to make
              sensible remarks,
    they ache
to express
              untamed feelings
        which melt
on your tongue
        with the taste
              of velvet thunder.

At the most
startling
              moments
    they insist
        on expressing

the revelations
            of madwomen,
                    the slow joy
    of tortoises,
the dialects
            of talking drums.

    Faced
                with numbness,
they spring
            extravagantly
    from dark
                chanting forests
into your dreams
            to speak out
through
    the voicebox
                of your longing.

Warrior

I have a new brace:
with it I can
    chew metal,
hang by my teeth
    from a helicopter,
catch bullets
    whistling through air
and in glistening moonlight
    scare the one-eyed werewolf.

I have new school shoes:
with them I can stride
    through marshes,
cross from continent
    to continent without tiring,
hop from Monday morning
    till Sunday evening non-stop
and squash armoured tanks
    with a single stomp.

I have new glasses:
with them I can see
    through steel doors,
decipher alien scripts
    and teachers' handwriting,
read the warning signs
    on exploding missiles,
and pierce the inscrutable gaze
    of enemies.

The other kids
won't notice,
will they?

A Caged Bird in Thailand

Please set this bird free.
It will bring you happy heart
and much prosperity.
Open cage costs ten baht.

This bird belongs to sky.
Why she prisoned in bamboo?
See wings twitching wide
for spread out sun and moon.

This bird hatched along pond.
Her daddy a busy hunting fellow.
Scavenged food for his little one
to make wing-feathers grow.

This bird has fresh memory.
Her head sweet with green fields.
She sings for her old country.
Lonely for her many friends.

This wild one made me run plenty.
Squawked and made wings flap.
Hard to snatch bird to city
and keep her alive in trap.

This creature captured too long.
Spirit feeble from one sad space.
But good-time bird still young.
With pretty feathers and face.

Please set this poor bird free.
It will bring you happy heart
and much prosperity.
Open cage costs ten baht.

Day Out

I don't want to go.
I'd rather stay in London.
My sister Julie also doesn't want to go.
But Mum and Tony want a day out.

We sit for hours cooped up
in the back seat of the car.
Behind us Coco drools with excitement.
I play my Gameboy all the way.

We arrive at this place
on the banks of a wide estuary.
Coco leaps out and within seconds
she's rolling in gloopy mud.

Out on the water are boats
and windsurfers riding the wind.
Tony takes photos of the beach huts
because they're on stilts.

Coco chases seagulls.
Julie collects shells.
Mum takes off her shoes and paddles.
I sit near a rock pool playing Tetris.

We eat our picnic lunch.
The wind blows sand in our faces.
Now I know why they're called sandwiches!
After lunch we go for a walk.

Tony takes photos of an old boat.
All that's left of it is its ribcage.
Julie collects a bag of seaweed
and wood that's been bleached by the sea.

Mum finds this cliff with small caves
hollowed out in the side of it.
She wants to climb to the top.
Coco bounds up ahead of her.

Tony follows after them.
They wave to us from up there.
Then Mum gives Tony a juicy hug.
I bet he'll move in soon.

I climb into one of the caves.
It's sheltered from the wind.
On the back wall it says: Spike woz ere.
It's a good place to play Tetris.

On the top of the ridge
we find a field of blackberries.
There's millions of them.
Mum asks us all to help her pick them.

We collect three bags full.
Our hands are stained bluish red
and so are our mouths and tongues
from all we've eaten.

Mum says she'll make blackberry pie
when we get back home.
And she'll freeze the rest
to eat in the middle of next winter.

This part of the river is deserted.
We're the only people around.
Coco starts barking at something
swimming in the water.

Whatever it is swims towards us.
It has dark glistening eyes
and looks at us inquisitively.
It's a solitary seal!

I wonder why this seal
has swum all the way up here
just to take a look at us.
I'm glad it has, though.

Tony tries to take a photo of it
but the seal is shy and swims away.
Back at the car
we have to dry Coco with a towel.

To tell the truth, she stinks.
On the way back to London
Julie makes a collage
out of seaweed, wood and shells.

Mum drives and Tony sleeps
with his head leaning against the window.
I get out my Gameboy
and play Tetris with blue fingers.

Kite-Flying

A sky
a breeze
a kite
a ball of string.

Wonder of wonders!
It flies
serenely –
you are in touch
with heaven.

Good Mother Lizard

While strolling through the grasslands
of the twentieth century we stumbled
into a crater which wasn't extraordinary

until we realized it was a scooped-out
mud-nest containing fifteen fossilized
baby dinosaurs each one meter long.

They weren't newborn but still occupied
the nest, waiting for mother to feed them.
On closer inspection, we found hundreds

of whole or broken eggs and the skeletons
of hatchlings and fully-grown, which told
a story of belonging and family feeling.

Nearby we found other nests: an entire
breeding colony of duck-billed dinosaurs,
grouped for protection against predators

like a modern-day community of penguins.
Painstakingly we put together the pieces
of the puzzle: powerful jaws for grinding

leaves and cones from Late Cretaceous
flowering plants and trees; fine-boned
hands; strong hind legs; flat tails.

Soon the lovable baby Maiasaur sprang
to life, complete with bark and grunt.
We could see it after birth, thriving

in the next, cared for by its parents
until old enough to roam with the herd.
Later, it may have joined the migration

to warmer regions during the winters.
Though a land-dweller, we could see it
swimming with side-to-side tail motion

to escape the old enemy Tyrannosaurus Rex,
using its acute vision, excellent hearing
and keen sense of smell to survive.

Yes, in that mud-nest we stumbled across
a long lost world without cities, without
humans, where creatures were small-brained

but larger than life, where each hour
took a million years and where the first
stirrings of tenderness evolved.

Chinese Whispers

It all started

when Jill's best friend Rachel mentioned to Melanie
that she saw Jill talking to Dick
who's much older than her.

Melanie (who can't keep her mouth shut) blabbed to Emma
about Jill going out with Rick
who must be at least sixteen because he's left school.

Emma (who never liked Jill) burst a lung
telling Debbie (the gossip queen)
that someone had seen Jill having it off with Nick
who's seventeen and on a training scheme.

Debbie couldn't wait to shoot her mouth off to Selma
(and you know what Selma's mind is like)
that Jill was probably going too far with Mick
who's over eighteen and works for Winston's, the builders.

Selma drivelled on to Rebecca
that if Jill was pregnant, then Mike,
a nineteen-year-old trainee manager, must be the father.

Rebecca (yakkety-yak) broadcast the news to Lizzy
that Jill would probably have to marry Mark.

Lizzy (who pokes her nose into everything)
let Shareen know that Mack
would never marry Jill because he fancied
her older sister's friend, Charlotte,
and anyway, he'd been made redundant.

The way Jill's mum heard the story

she was in dead trouble,
five months pregnant,
and desperate to get married.
The father, Jack,
twenty-two-years old,
was a drunken layabout
who had vanished to another town
because he didn't want
the responsibility.

Starving on TV

I am small as a puppet
but with no strings
and made entirely of light.

I am thinner than paper
with pitiless black flies
speckling my enormous head.

I am one of a hundred
million clones
that can be exterminated

at the press of a button.
I used to be a child
but now I'm just an image.

No one knows my name.
Only the unnatural
swollenness of my belly

will be remembered,
the grim emptiness
of my eyes,

the spider-print
of my ribcage
against my skin,

and these bulbous joints
on my fleshless limbs.
I am the unwelcome visitor

in your living rooms.
I stare out from my box
at your palatial homes.

Sometimes you are too busy
with your snacks
to notice my hunger.

At other times you're laughing
and having fun
with your comical red noses.

Only rarely do I make
eye contact with you
and exchange tears.

Perhaps next time you see me
I will be a lifeless bundle
wrapped in rags.

Gull

A seagull can sit
where I can't:
on top of the spindliest
chimney in our road.

She squawks so raucously
each morning
I wake from dreams
of iron doors clanking.

This particular seagull
is a great one for gossiping.
She broadcasts her programme
of news for hours on end.

Her silhouette
against the morning sun
is that of a plump,
overweight duck.

But when she rises in flight
with her wings spread
she's more graceful than an angel
because she's real.

I don't know where she spends
the warm afternoons
but each morning she gives
the chimney her soft shape.

Perhaps she flies
over the glistening sea
keeping track of fat fish
beneath the surface.

Or is she one of those
who trails in the slipstream
of ferries scavenging
its cast-off muck? I hope not.

Luckily she wasn't the embalmed bird
I found on the beach
which had been spat out
of the sea's mouth.

Electronic Brain

I am an intelligent machine:
I read *Computer Weekly* magazine.
    My ancestors were robotic,
    their procedures idiotic –
with not much going on behind the screen.

I am an intelligent machine:
everything I say I really mean.
    My dictionary's extensive,
    my grammar's comprehensive,
I'm never flummoxed by the unforseen.

I am an intelligent machine:
my program lets me vary my routine.
    I think it's prejudicial
    to call me artificial –
I can tell you who I am and where I've been.

I am an intelligent machine:
my processors are bug-free and serene.
    I have friendly interfaces,
    gigantic databases . . .
Oops! FATAL ERROR: MEMORY WIPED CLEAN.

Friends

1

Trevor often talked to Sue
under the oak tree. They'd be
together for the whole of break.
And the bell would ring too soon.

She seemed to want his company
more than the others. He liked
the Bounty bars she shared with him.
During class they'd try to work

together or in the same group.
She laughed at jokes so he learned
as many as he could. And riddles.
She was good with her hands.

She made a model yacht from a kit.
The sail was transparent plastic
with stick-on stripes. It floated
elegantly on the sunlit lake.

He walked her home that afternoon.
She lived next to the Red Lion
and hers was the narrow house
almost hidden by ivy leaves.

2

One autumn morning Sue was absent
from school. Trevor played soccer
with his mates. He was goalie
and carelessly let one in.

After lunch Josh informed him
that Sue's father had died
the day before. He was at work
when he just fell down dead.

Trevor felt awful. He imagined Sue
crying in her house veiled with ivy.
Trevor's own father was healthy
and belonged to a cycle club.

Was Sue's father much older?
She stayed away for a week.
Trevor heard that she'd gone
to her father's funeral.

3

At night Trevor had trouble
falling asleep. He was bothered
by images. When Sue returned
to school she looked depressed.

She stared a lot, at nothing
in particular. And at breaktime,
Trevor avoided the oak tree.
He wouldn't know what to say to her.

He was fearful of the emptiness
which had opened up between them.
She didn't do much in class.
Trevor hung around with his mates.

Sue didn't talk to him and he
didn't talk to her. He found out
that her father wasn't old at all
when he died. It was a heart attack.

Trevor worried about his own father.
How could someone die so suddenly?
One time Sue was standing alone
in the corridor when Trevor came by.

They saw each other. For a moment
he nearly stopped to speak to her.
But he walked faster and she turned
her eyes away. He didn't look back.

4
Trevor didn't know which project
to choose. He wondered which
Sue would choose. She sat near
the window staring out at the sky.

Trevor noticed her using a hand
to wipe away tears from her eyes.
So did Miss Jenkins who went over
and put her arms around Sue.

Trevor decided on river pollution.
He scribbled a note to Sue asking
if she'd like to do river pollution
with him. Then he wrote a PS:

'I'm sorry about your dad.'

Yesterday, Today and Tomorrow

Yesterday I chanted the seal-song
with sailors who were departing.
I said goodbye to friends
who were spellbound in their star-lit towers.
I watched the distant cities burn.

Today I speak to an eagle in eagle-language
while I fly on its back.
I eat berries from the bush that Merlin planted.
I sleep high up in a tree
whose branches support the universe.

Tomorrow I will be Emperor of the Islands
where the feathered Paggalagoes live.
I will defeat the Muckdragon
with my dagger that shimmers in the dark
and walk my dog on the rings of Saturn.

The Move

My old room,
snug as a broom cupboard,
was where I felt at home.

The berries of the rowan tree
tapped on my windows
like good neighbours.

Streets were dotted
with friends pedalling
to and from each other's houses.

Teachers knew us by name
and in the supermarket
asked about our zebra-finches.

My mother was happy
in those days
and warmed the winter evenings
with a gas log-fire.

Water

Before this water
    offered itself
        to my thirst
it was snow
    on the Himalayas.
        When melted
it frolicked
    down the slopes
        between villages,
became the Ganges
    that lapped the feet
        of Holy Men.
Majestically
    it swept through
        the multitudinous
plains of India
    before merging
        into the salty ocean
of jewelled fish.
    Here it hauled
        oil-tankers
and whaling factories
    on its shoulders
        before evaporating
into the lofty air.

Before this water
    flowed to me
        through a labyrinth
of pipes,
    it rained down
        on the armour-plating
of an armadillo
    in the Amazon jungle.
        On the dank earth
it served
    the rotting of leaves,
        was sucked
into the roots
    of a giant fig tree.
        As sap it rose
to the heights
    of forest canopy,
        became flower
and vied
    for the courtship of bees.
        Finally it swelled
into fruit
    and was selected
        by the beak
of an ostentatious toucan.

Before this water
     gurgled
          down my throat
it was cradled
     in the folds
          of a storm cloud
to Africa,
     where it darkened
          the earth below
and exploded
     thunderously.
          This water
added extra ferocity
     to the flood
          that swept away
a village,
     before it joined
          the mighty Zambezi
and passed through
     the mouth of a hippo.
          At the Victoria Falls
it vaporized
     into a mist
          which held rainbows
in its embrace.

Before this water
    became substance
        of my body
it seeped through
    permeable rocks
        to the water table
where it slumbered
    beneath the hills.
        In a sudden burst
of generosity
    it gushed upwards
        in bubbling springs
and fountains
    to be sloshed
        through the dishwashers
and washing machines
    of Berlin,
        Rome and Paris.
It irrigated farms
    in Spain and England
        and when I'm
done with it,
    who knows where
        this water
will journey next?

The Sorry Puppet

Dear Mum,
I'm sorry sorry sorry.
Sorry for cutting your dress
into little pieces.

I'm a puppet
that's out of control.
My hands are sorry.
My fingers are sorry.

Sorry for putting
salt in your sugar.
It won't ever happen again.
Sorry I screamed at you.

My mouth is sorry.
My tongue is sorry.
And whoever was working
my strings is sorry.

Sorry for stealing
money from your purse.
I'm sorry sorry sorry.
Sorry I kicked you.

My legs are sorry.
My feet are sorry.
But now I've decided
to work my own strings.

Sorry for telling lies
about Jessica.
Sorry for hiding
your perfume.

My head is sorry.
My heart is sorry.
And I hope you'll give me
one more chance.

So my puppet can learn
a different dance.
I'm sorry, Mum.
Really sorry.

The Goldfish Plant

The plant we bought
at the jumble sale
with its shrivelled stalk
like a firework fuse

idled away its first years
on the kitchen sill.
But when we moved it
to the bathroom

it exploded
into a cluster
of green tentacles
trailing from the pot.

Unexpectedly
it spawned orange eggs
along the length
of its abundant tendrils

and before we had time
to be astonished
these hatched –
into goldfish!

Such a furious blossoming
of golden light,
but attached
to the mother plant

by their tails.
With gawping mouths
sucking desperately
at the air,

they struggled
to unstick themselves.
Then it happened:
after two days

the first goldfish
swam free,
followed by others
eager for the world.

Soon the stalks
were an abandoned green.
And the fish swam
through the rooms

of our house,
bright and airy,
swimming into our dreams
and our conversations.

Golden shoals
carrying their light
into caves and crannies
between furniture.

We were privileged
that they had selected
our eccentric house
as their abode.

Visitors never ceased
to be amazed: they came
from far and wide
to see for themselves.

Some brought cameras.
But no one succeeded
in capturing these ethereal
goldfish on film.

The open-minded, however,
went away satisfied
with impossible airfish
swimming in their heads.

Snap, Crackle, Pop

Wake up sunshine, morning treat,
don't leave home before you eat,
hearty breakfast, fortified,
free collect-a-cards inside,

protein, energy, sodium, vitamin,
niacin, fibre, calcium, thiamin,
sugar, glucose, chocolate, malt,
yummy honey, marshmallow, salt,

barley (ground),
bran (baked),
wheat (shredded),
corn (flaked),

family, first established, milling,
children, growing, vital, filling,
energy, daily, wholesome, nutritious,
natural, low-fat, balanced, delicious,

pecan, coconut, almond, sultana,
apple, hazelnut, date, banana,
papaya, apricot, maple, strawberry,
pineapple, sunflower, sesame, cherry,

oats (rolled),
rice (toasted),
raisins (splitzed),
nuts (roasted),

special offers, details on the back,
trademark, tokens, two per pack,
cut-out dinosaurs, space-glo-stickers,
genuine Matchbox die-cast replicas,

aprons, calculators, magic stencils,
wicked watches, coloured pencils,
new-look package, recycled, green,
by appointment to the Queen,

nuggets, loops, pillows, hearts,
clusters, rings, puffs, tarts,
Malties, Crispies, Shreddies, Munchies,
Toasties, Frosties, Sweeties, Crunchies.

Night Terrors

I've forgotten how to sleep.
It used to come naturally
when the streetlight shone
its muzzy yellow
through the gap in my curtains.

But now as I try to doze off
I keep hearing noises of skirmish.
It could be my imagination
except for the Ford
on its back next morning.

I hear bricks through the window.
Ever since it happened to old
Mrs Dalla who lives on her own
in the end terrace
my sleep is splintered with glass.

I recognized one of the gang
who scrawled swearwords over
the whitewashed walls of number 27.
He's the same bloke
who stoned my streetlight.

I've forgotten how to sleep.
It used to come naturally
when I curled up into a ball
of innocent dreams.
But now night is a bully.

Mythic Animals

No creature
is more astonishing
than the unicorn
with its magical spiral horn

unless it's a crab
with six pairs of jaws
sideways scuttle
and eyes at the ends of stalks

or perhaps a bat
with membrane between
its elongated fingers
hanging upside-down like an umbrella

or a zebra
with its fingerprint face
and Newcastle United
football shirt

or a hummingbird
that can fly backwards
with wings vibrating
a hundred beats per second

or a dolphin
with Buddha smile
performing a series of aerial leaps
as if to say farewell.

The Moon in Leo

One day I intend to be an astrologer
and write things like: Jupiter in Libra
makes friendships blossom into love.

Or: Saturn, your ruling planet,
is helping you overcome your shyness,
but Mars in Cancer is causing havoc

with your emotional energies.
My boyfriend, Mark, thinks it's hogwash.
All he knows about stars is that they

are gorgeous and come from Hollywood.
But I believe they decide your future.
I tried it on my best friend, Janine.

She's a Virgo and a true romantic.
I checked out her chart and the stars
indicated that she would capture

the most droolsome guy within a week.
Venus will set your heart racing,
I wrote, and perk up your love life.

Wednesday at the club and Friday
at Joanne's party she was all smiles.
By Saturday night she was depressed –

the boy of her dreams hadn't showed up.
At midnight, though, I noticed her
in a clinch with a bloke in the dark.

And when she later told me astrology
was all hogwash, I knew it was Mark.
At home I compiled my own horoscope:

The mighty planet Pluto in Scorpio
provides you with plenty ammunition
to fight back for what you want.

Irksome

I loathe the hideous little Irk
who gets beneath my skin.
He practises his handiwork
upon me from within.

His tickling makes me go berserk
with every tweak and twitch.
His tiny ego gets a perk
each time I itch itch itch.

The little monster doesn't shirk
from torturing my sleep.
He must gain pleasure from his quirk
of making my flesh creep.

But watch out loathsome, hideous Irk,
it's time for your dispatch.
I'll wipe the face right off your smirk –
but first . . . just one more scratch!

Mountain Biking

You don't mind the morning being cold
as you coast out onto the open road,

light as a butterfly, strong as an eagle,
taking the first curve at the perfect angle,

winding through the canyons of Capel St Mary,
past the Happy Eater, down the precarious

shelf trail onto the lip of the A12
which is tough, cruel and mean as hell.

You veer off at the old Copdock single-track
and bullet down towards the cul-de-sac

with the wind ricocheting off your face.
Under the bridge you slam on brakes,

mount the kerb, and muscle up the path
with hairpin bends until you're out of breath.

Flanked by glaciated streams and gullies
which plunge into misty alpine valleys,

you reach the crest of the switchback
with its magnificent views of Tesco carpark.

Next comes the trek over mud, crud and goop,
then white-knuckled down a rock-infested slope

to the churning roundabout where you dodge
insane car-drivers going over the edge.

It's time to fuel up with your low-fat,
high-energy, optimum-performance chocolate

as you approach the centre of Ipswich.
This you know to be the most evil stretch

of your gruelling journey so you adopt
an aggressive ride position to boulder-leap

the traffic jams and bomb through the city
on your lightweight engineered geometry.

Because the fumes get right up your nose
you freely abandon the rat-race and choose

to hammer up the forbidden inclines
of Christchurch Park, via the tree-lined

avenues, cross-country to the high plateau,
surrounded by snow-capped summits which grow

in magnificence with each turn of the pedals.
You gladly pogo the jagged, yawning potholes

along the gravel short-cut through the morass
of suburbs until you join the hectic bypass.

Then it's a blazing finish down the fast lane,
the ultimate descent through craggy terrain,

including a last-minute slalom around
the vehicles parked in the school grounds,

to arrive, overheated, at your destination,
but only five minutes late for registration.

Newborn Child

I am not a Buddhist,
I am not Hindu,
I am not a Muslim —
but I'm just like you.

Just like you —
and you're just like me.
Inside there are no differences
for us to see.

I am not a Christian,
I am not a Jew,
I am not a Heathen —
but I'm just like you.

Just like you —
and you're just like me.
There isn't any simpler way
for us to be.